Hidden Miracles

An Epic Story Of How God Restored One Family Back To Him

I0151781

By

Earline Terrell Cameron

Hidden Miracles

An Epic Story Of How God Restored
One Family Back To Him

By:

Earline Terrell Cameron

Copyright@2015
All Rights Reserved
Printed in The United States of America

Published By:

ABM Publications

A division of Andrew Bills Ministries, Inc.
PO Box 6811, Orange, CA 92863
www.abmpublications.com

ISBN: 978-1-931820-55-4

All scripture quotations, unless otherwise indicated are taken from the King James Version of the Bible, Public Domain. All Rights Reserved

TABLE OF CONTENTS

	Acknowledgments	iii
	Introduction	1
1	Place Of Peace And Prosperity	5
2	The Fall	11
3	Place Of Poverty	17
4	Protection And Restoration	25
5	Learning To Trust	31
6	Angelic Protection	37
7	God Hears And Answers Prayer	43
8	Miracles Of Restoration And Healing	47
9	God's Protection	51
10	Provision And Growth	59
	Summary And Closing	65

HIDDEN MIRACLES

DEDICATION

This book is dedicated to my parents:

Hope and Zellie Terrell

EARLINE TERRELL CAMERON

ACKNOWLEDGMENTS

I am so thankful to God who has blessed me with the gifts, talents, and abilities to be a blessing to so many people, to share my story in hope that they too will be able to see and recognize the magnificent hand of The Lord working throughout their lives.

I thank my family for their love and support throughout the years.

I thank my publishing company.

·

HIDDEN MIRACLES

INTRODUCTION

I have learned that as the Bible says, "All things work together for good to them that love God, to them who are the called according to His purpose." (Romans 8:28) Therefore, all of the things that we go through are necessary for us. But one of the things that I did not know was that God is behind the scenes working miracles for us so that at the appointed time we can look back and see what He has been doing.

Most of us never get to the point in our journey with Christ where He shows us all of the miracles that He has been performing in our lives. We never look at Him as working behind the scenes for us. He wants to show us these things. He wants us to know the kind of God He is. He loves us so much.

I believe that God waited all of this time to show me the miracles that He had performed in my life because had He shown them to me sooner, I would not have appreciate them the way I do now. I saw these things happening, but I did not believe in miracles. I did not know much about God. I knew that I wanted to have a relationship with God, but I thought He would not care about little old me because He had too many people who were doing everything right and they were way. I felt that I was so insignificant to God. But I could not have been more I was wrong.

In 2008 I knew that I had heard the voice of God nudging me to write a book, but what He was telling me to do was something I felt was too much for me. He knew that I felt like I had led a boring life. He knew all of this and He knew what I would say. I told Him I didn't know how to write a book and I didn't think I had anything to say. It seems that after I had answered that within myself the idea sort of went on hold. I have since learned that whenever God commands us to do something, He has already made the provision for us to do the assignment! It was not until February of 2012 when God pulled the shutters off my eyes, spiritually speaking, that I was able to see everything that He wanted me to talk about in this book. God started to open my understanding and I began to realize He had done miracle after miracle in my life! That is what has inspired me to want to share about all He has done for my family and me over the years. This revelation from God was so significant in my life.

My intention with this book is to stimulate your imagination with inspiration about your own miracles that God has performed throughout your life. As the Holy Spirit sat me down and showed me how He had made provision for my family all of my life, I was blown away. But it is not until you get to that place in worshipping Him that He will show you things that have gone on behind the scenes.

The fact of the matter is that God wants all of us to walk in our destiny, therefore throughout our lives He has been performing miracles strategically for us and our families. He does not just want to save us, He wants to save our entire family.

At one time in my life I was just walking around aimlessly, not having a clue as to what was really going on in my life. Some of you may feel that way today, but I am here to tell you there is a war going on in the spirit realm.

The enemy of our souls is trying to stop God's people from reaching their destiny. The devil knows that if you ever get a revelation as to who you are in Christ, and all of the miracles God has been performing on your behalf, he has lost you and you will never walk around aimlessly again! Instead, you will *know* that God is real and He is the Rewarder of those who diligently seek Him, and you will have a life full of focus. We have to seek God in order to find Him. He only reveals Himself to those who are serious about their walk with Him.

I think that all of us have a book inside of us. If you are a child of God and He speaks to you, He will show you the miracles that He has performed in your life, even the things that at the time you did not give enough thought to, never actually realizing that situation was a miracle. If you ask Him to, God will pull the scales off your eyes so that you will be able to see it as you look back on things.

When I was a young girl in church I used to hear the pastor and deacons say "it takes a made up mind". I really did not get it then. I have thought about it as a grown-up, but it was not until I truly made my own mind up that I was able to clearly understand what that phrase really means. You have to be fully sold out for Jesus. It is when you "know that you know" that He is real, that He is the only true and living God; when you know that you can do nothing without Him; When you know that He is your God, when you know that He is with you, and that nothing else matters, the house, the car, people, no one matters but Him. You get to the point where you put no one before Him. When all you want is Him and His Presence, when you don't want to live without Him, you are then finally at the point where you begin to understand what they meant when they would make the statement, "It takes a made up mind."

Today I just want to encourage someone to not give up, that God is truly not finished with you yet. Many times I wanted to give up, throw in the towel, but God would bring me out, yet another time. He was and still is molding me, pruning me, shaping me into what He has called me to be. It is all about Him. He is the Potter, I am the clay. He wants us to come to the end of ourselves, and He will be right there waiting with outstretched arms.

This book is about the miracles that God has performed in my life. It does contain and mention all of the miracles that God has performed in my life and the lives of some of my family members.

When God has put a call on your life, it didn't just happen when you realized it. That call was put on your life before the foundation of the world! I had to come to this realization because that was one of my questions early on. When did God actually start calling me?

Chapter One

PLACE OF PEACE AND PROSPERITY

As a young girl growing up in the Mississippi Delta, the spring season was the most beautiful time of the year. I loved the spring, it seemed as if everything was good, everything was beautiful. The leaves were blossoming, you could smell new pine needles and flowers budding; the air was filled with different fragrances – scents of lilacs, daffodils, tulips, and especially the magnolias! My grandfather (Papa) had many fruit trees and bushes. I used to love the smell of them all, including the berries. So by this you can tell I love the springtime in Mississippi.

With everything growing, spring was a time when there was new life emerging on the scene. This would also be a favorite time for me because as a child growing up in that little brown shotgun house, the spring was a time of plenty. We planted a huge garden every year. My dad and mom would let us help them plant the garden. We had corn, peas, butter beans, cucumber, watermelon, cantaloupe, okra, tomatoes, upper ground potatoes, red potatoes, and squash. We had plenty in this place. I remember feeling really secure in this house.

All was well in the spring that year. We picked all the wonderful vegetables in order to be canned. I watched my mom can the food and put it in mason jars as I did every year as far back as I could remember. It was so fascinating to me to watch her cook and label the food and put it all in these jars for the winter months when food was so scarce and when Dad could not get work. But I have come to realize that God was showing me the difference in this place.

I learned a lot at an early age being in this place. My other siblings did not have a clue about the things I was learning. I did not know what was going on, but I knew when the change happened. If you were to ask any of my siblings when did the change come for your family financially or as it came down to having enough to eat, they could not tell you because I believe God chose me to be a blessing to my family. Hence, I had to have the understanding of what was going on to be able to look back and see what He was doing and to be able to bless others.

My parents had eleven children together. However, my father had been married before he met my mother. Therefore, we have an older sister who was not raised with us but nevertheless, we are all sisters and brothers. I am one of the middle children. My parents had a rough time raising eleven children. A lot of times they had to make a lot of sacrifices, but throughout the years my parents would often tell us that the year that I was born was the worst year of all. I was born in January. It was cold and a lot of times they did not have food! I was probably hungry as a baby just like my older sisters and my brother, but they'd had hard times before, so they knew how to get through it. The year that they always reflected upon as being the toughest, however, was the year that I was born. I used to laugh at it when they talked about it, because I did not know certain things about myself then, but as I matured in Christ, God has revealed to me that the enemy was trying to take me out, even back then as a baby. I was told food was so scarce and the north wind in Mississippi was no joke, but praise be to God, He watched over us, protected us, kept us alive and together, and brought us through those hard times.

The economic situation in Mississippi during the 1950's and most of the 1960's and even into the '70's for the most part was horrible. So when you don't know much about God and how He deals with people or about how to get in the will of God, you stay stuck in poverty. For my parents, school was not a top priority. They made sure that we went to school, but they had very little education themselves.

When I was eleven years old the Lord began to show me that in the spring and summer we had plenty and in the winter months we barely had enough to eat. My mom would can food for the winter months so that we would have enough food. It all worked okay while we were in the brown shotgun style house, but when we had to move from that place it was not good at all.

We were hungry a lot of days. I remember one day my dad was at work on the tractor in the field. My mom took us with her to her job where she had to iron for a Caucasian lady who lived in a big white house. We had no idea that we would have to stay in the car for as long as we did, but however long it took her to iron that lady's clothes, we were in that car! Around lunchtime my mom brought us some food to eat and after that we still had to wait for her to finish more ironing. I think my mom brought us with her because we had no food at home, so she did not want to leave us there with nothing to eat. It is so amazing what a mother will do for her children. So if a mother will go to those lengths for her children, can you imagine what God would do for His children!

Also at the age of eleven, I gave my life to Christ. Mind you, I really did not know what that meant at the time. I was on the "Mourner's Bench" in church, praying for God to forgive me of my sins, to save me and my family and other things that a child of eleven years old would pray. For two weeks other people and I were on the "Mourner's Bench" in our little small Baptist Church. I have since learned that this "Mourner's Bench" tradition was started in the late 1700's when we had a great revival period in America, people were urged to come to the front of the church, get on the "Mourner's Bench" and repent, seeking God for forgiveness and salvation. It was popular during the time of D.L. Moody and Charles Finney, well-known preachers and evangelists back in the day.

This was my second year sitting on the bench. It was the second week of the revival on a Wednesday. The preacher kept telling us to take the chair. I kept praying trying to keep my mind on God. I think I knew that I would take the chair that night; it was as if it was planned in advance, so I took the chair that Wednesday night. I got baptized that Sunday morning. I felt really good about it.

When I got baptized that started this urge inside of me to always pray for my family. I believe God called me to pray for my family even back then. I don't believe my father was praying because he did not go to church. My mom prayed. She was a Christian and she made sure all of us went to church every Sunday and even Sunday school.

My grandfather was a deacon in the church, and he

was well respected by many people. He and my step-grandmother went to church every Sunday. My grandfather used to pray a lot and people used to like to hear his prayers. I think God was with him until he started rubbing elbows with the wrong people. So I have a spiritual background of having older relatives who prayed and believed in God.

When I gave my life to Christ one Wednesday night, my mom shouted. It shocked me. I wondered why she was shouting. I had heard the Spirit tell me to get up and take the chair, so I did. But I think the Holy Spirit was telling my mother something different. How many of us knew that when we make a step toward God all of Heaven is watching, as well as the enemy and his fallen angels?

I think God really had to let me know that we were blessed and what happened to get us out of the will of God, and what we had to pray and repent from so that we would be back in the will of God as a family.

EARLINE TERRELL CAMERON

Chapter Two

THE FALL

I remember my dad joining a group of some sort. I knew very little about them, but I thought it meant my dad would have friends now. I remember he came home one night with a bandaged area on his chest and there was a little blood. I was afraid for him. Soon after that we had to move from the little brown shotgun house. My mom and dad sold all of the chickens. I was hurt about that. We moved in to a small white bungalow-type house about two miles away on a different road. The brown shotgun house with the huge garden had been a place of plenty, even though in the winter it would get rough, but I could sense something wasn't quite right. There was a shift of some sort, I was just too young to understand. I would miss that brown house and having plenty of food to eat, at least for a large part of the time.

I feel that we were out of the will of God because no one was praying and my father and grandfather were rubbing elbows with a satanic group of people. Our food source started to diminish. We didn't have the garden anymore, which was so vital for our survival. The chickens were gone, sold for a mere 10 dollars at that time. Even at eleven years old, I knew something was very wrong with that price, but they needed the money to move and where we were going there was no chicken coup anyway.

As all this was happening and I watched my world change, I knew we were in trouble. My family had fallen out of the will of God. There are consequences for these actions. My father and grandfather thought they were doing a good thing which made them look like they had some clout, but that was not so when it came to God. I believe the impact of some of their choices ran deep for years to come.

The Bible tells us there is a way that seems right unto a man, but the end thereof is the way of death. First Thessalonians 5:18 tells us "In everything give thanks, for this is God's will for you in Christ Jesus." Dad was not giving thanks to God for what he had. I do remember my dad getting baptized after I did, but I am not sure what happened within his heart. I want to believe that he gave his life to Christ and repented for what he had done, he and my grandfather. But the effects of what they had done were already started and in progress, therefore, in order to reverse the curse, someone had to be used by God to pray the right prayer.

Whatever ungodly prayer that was prayed over my family, whether knowingly or unknowing, had a big effect on the males in my family. My parents had four sons and not even one of them was or is successful. And to take that to another level the next generation of males was having the same problem until, glory be to God; The Holy Spirit helped me to see in just the last few years what the problem was and what I needed to do to reverse that curse that had been assigned to the males in my family. Before praying that prayer of restoration for my family the future of my family looked very dim, but now praise God the sky is the limit! Within the last four years we have males and females in this family who are in college and are in the top of their class. But as I look back I tried to present the problem to my sisters and a brother but they at that time did not see anything wrong in the family they felt that everyone make their own choices. So basically, no one else believes in Generational Curses. I was only 10 or 11 years old when I was able to see that something was happening. I did not know what was happening, but in my spirit I knew something was going on. But praise be to God, The Holy Spirit connected me to a good bible-based church where I began to study the bible and learn more about God and His will for my life.

I have four brothers. My oldest brother was a good athlete. He was a fast runner on the track team at his high school. His coaches loved him there was no way he should have ended up the way that he did. Everyone believed there was a scholarship in his future. But when there are spiritual forces working against a strong, extremely talented athlete even he will not be able to prevail. My brother quit school in the eleventh grade, one year prior to graduating, and went to Florida to work a job picking oranges. He ended up getting in trouble with the law, and was sent to prison for ten years. He was later on heroine, as well as heavy alcohol use which led to various degenerative diseases and he passed away at age 62. My second brother, my father's namesake, passed away at the age of 60. He inherited my father's congestive heart disease. He did not graduate from high school, as a matter of fact he did not like school growing up as a kid. Later on as we grew up, he and I would be in a conversation about something and would say to myself wow! What if this young man had continued to further his education, he was very knowledgeable on almost any subject that was brought up. I loved him dearly and he knew it, but he had a weakness for drugs as my oldest brother did.   What he could not do academically his daughter and grandson are doing.   His daughter has graduated from a major university having earned her Master's Degree, and her son is in his second year at the University of Chicago.   Our God hears prayers and He is a merciful God.

My third brother was not successful either, He got married and started to go to church, got saved, and was doing well and I often enjoyed talking to him about his religion. He and his wife became very involved in God's work. They moved to a neighboring state and I don't really know what happened to their marriage. I do know that the marriage ended, which was traumatic to their family, their five children suffered the most. Apparently drugs had become a daily part of my brother's life.   I have the hope that God can do anything but fail, so I continue to pray for this brother and believe that he will rededicate his life to The Lord and work on rebuilding that relationship between him and God.

My youngest brother was very athletic, he played football and also baseball. My parents were so proud of him. They went to every one of his games and encouraged him. He was a very good athlete and should have been very successful. He received a scholarship to MVS University. I don't really know what happened there, but it seemed to me that he was afraid of something. Maybe there was too much pressure, I'm not sure. He stayed there a year, then he wanted to go to a two-year college instead. He did make that change, but then he dropped out and got a job working on the highways and roads. We tried to get him in at Long Beach State in California, but it did not go well. He found a security job and he worked there and sent for his family to come out to live with him.

A few years later it seemed as though family life was too much for him. He stated having mental problems and it was downhill from there on. To make a long story short, my four brothers seemed to each have issues, and every time they got to a place where they were about to be a success story or get a good job or opportunity, or in my brother's case, become a great athlete, there seemed to be a ceiling or something there keeping them from going any farther above that. It was and still is a sad thing to see, to watch each of them try to reach success and yet watch it be sabotaged somehow. It was that generational curse that stopped his success as a top Football player. But as with my other brother, I continue to pray for this brother to repent and give his life to Christ.

I think that because of the spiritual situation in our family, the boys did not have a chance. Because of praying and knowing what to pray for, I believe the ceiling that plagued my brothers is no longer there. Now the sky is the limit for my own sons and grandsons and even my great grandsons, so faith and prayer to God are the only way to get rid of generational curses and begin a new pattern of generational blessings instead!

EARLINE TERRELL CAMERON

Chapter Three

PLACE OF POVERTY

-- The Miracle Meal --

It was a regular Saturday morning, no school, everybody was home except my mom. Dad was not supposed to be home, but because of the weather he could not work. Everybody got up one by one, went into the kitchen like people do when you wake up in the morning. I think I had gone in there twice just to make sure there was absolutely nothing in the kitchen to eat. We were used to breakfast because in the past mom would get up early, cook grits and bacon, or something like that for us, but not this morning. She was gone to work and she knew that we had nothing to eat. I wanted to cry. The sad thing is, we knew she would not be home soon because she was cleaning somebody's house or ironing for them.

After everyone had taken a "tour" of the kitchen, even my dad, I was really feeling bad. When I passed by my dad he said "Lene, go in the kitchen and cook somethin'." I looked at him and I could not believe he was asking me to cook something. My oldest sister in the house was sixteen years old, she was a majorette in the band at school. My other sister was fourteen years old, she loved to read. I was the next daughter in the house and was twelve years old by that time. I had never cooked anything! I used to watch my mom cook sometimes, but I was most familiar with the canning. So when my dad asked me to cook I honestly did not know what to do! I didn't see anything to cook either. But how many of us know that when God wants to work a miracle through you, you don't have to know how or what to do? He will show you what to do, and turn nothing into something! He just needs a willing and obedient person and a little flour and water to make the world's best tasting gravy and hotcakes.

When dad asked me to go in the kitchen and cook something, I looked at him for a moment, then said. "Okay." I had no idea what to do. I looked in the cupboards. On the table all I saw was white flour and lard. Don't ask me how I did it, because to this day I don't really know, but I made some gravy. It was the best tasting gravy that I have been able to make. I have not been able to imitate it to this day! I have tried over the years. I made some hotcakes too (for those who don't know what hotcakes are, it's just bread made on top of the stove). That bread was so good! All God needs is a little bit of something, and then He will multiply it so everyone will be fed and have some left over!

When I finished cooking I fixed dad's plate for him; he was just smacking his lips, and he said, "Lene, this is so good!" It is not that the food was so good because we were starving, we weren't. We had eaten the night before, but when you get up in the morning, most people are hungry, so you look for food to eat. The gravy and bread was so good, my sisters and I talked about it down through the years! That was the first miracle that I remember God working for my family, even though I had not looked at it as a miracle back then, since I knew nothing about miracles. I actually did not know much about God!

-- Prayer for Restored Looks and Self-Esteem --

At age eleven, I looked relatively nice and I thought that I was cute. I had just started "blossoming" as a young lady so I was growing up and heading into puberty. At age twelve, my facial features started changing. I found myself very unattractive and I was so hurt and my self-esteem hit a low that I had not seem before. Keep in mind that at eleven years old I was attractive all was going well, after all I had given my life to Jesus and I felt good. I was learning to pray and it was a good season in my life. So be it not strange that one year later, (12 years old), the enemy steps in and tries to make me the most miserable person on planet Earth. So I started praying for God to restore my looks. I became very shy and withdrawn I tried not to look at people in their face if I did not have to.

The summer after I turned thirteen, I was used to the idea of being unattractive. I felt that God was not hearing my prayers, but I continued to pray in spite of not seeing any real change. I was almost afraid to look at people because my self-esteem was so low. (I remember when I took my school picture at age twelve, my teacher looked at it and she could only say that I had pretty white teeth. I recall being very embarrassed because the picture was so horrible!)

During that summer I got closer to God. I read my Bible continually. At age fourteen I started looking better, I started feeling better as well. I started writing songs and I would send these songs off to music companies, I remember this one music company because their name is so imbedded in my memory but I am not sure if I can mention their name in this book. But at age fourteen I feel that God has heard my prayers and I was looking better. At age fifteen I felt that God had totally healed me from that situation. I praise God for being there with me every step of the way. He was teaching me to trust Him that He would be with me because His word says He will never leave us nor forsake us. (Heb. 13:5) This was when God put in my heart to write. I feel that yes God was teaching me to trust Him, but it was a twofold blessing because from this situation a passion to write was developing inside of me, even though I only wanted to write songs. See my Heavenly Father knew that one day I would have to write this book and in order to do that I needed the gift inside of me. I am just amazed at how God thinks of everything!

When I look back, I think in my mind the white house represented a place of poverty, a place where we would have to rely on God for everything. It should have been a place for my entire family to pray and get closer to God, but it seemed that no one got it. I was forced to pray because I had always prayed for my family, but would I continue to pray and trust God in this place where there was nothing?

While at the white house we had a fig tree in the back yard that never bore fruit. I would check that tree for figs every year until we moved. Never once did that tree bore fruit. I know that there is a story in the bible where Jesus cursed the fig tree that had no fruit on it. (Matt. 21:19) But I kid you not, we had a fig tree that was barren the whole time we lived there, and guess what no one live in that house after we moved. When we moved the house stayed empty until the owner tour it down the next year or so. The house went so did the fig tree! That was so frustrating, because the tree could have been a source of food. It seemed as if that tree had a poverty mentality!

- Wishing For A Best Friend -

I remember when I started coming of age around twelve or thirteen or thereabouts I wanted a friend or a boyfriend. Mostly I wanted a friend. I would do anything for a friend. I settled for a puppy, because I couldn't find a friend. My first puppy died, actually he froze to death after the snow fell one night. For some reason that puppy was afraid of me and wouldn't ever come to me. The next puppy I got was afraid of me also. All I wanted to do was to cuddle them and be their friend. The first puppy was jet black, the second puppy was light brown. The second puppy got hit by a car in the road. I was so hurt in my heart both times. So I was left needing a friend but couldn't find one. I'd had such high hopes about both puppies, but that just didn't work out.

It seemed to me that good friends were hard to come by. So, I sought out to find a good friend at school. I remember my mom would get up early in the morning and cook our breakfast before we went to school. We would eat breakfast, and then she would give us ten cents. if she had it, and that was for our lunch. Then when we got home we would eat. Well, I met a new friend at school and I asked her if she had lunch money. She told me "no". She came from a really poor family, so I would give her one of my nickels since I had two. In a sense I paid for friendship by sharing my lunch money with her to be my friend. I was a needy person. That girl and I were friends that first year, but she wasn't a very good friend because friends stick by you through thick and thin, and don't laugh at you behind your back. Friends should "have your back", not talk behind your back! So, that friendship was over.

The next year I met another friend, and her family was even poorer than the first friend's was! So I would give her a nickel of my money every day, just like I had done the year before with the first friend. Then I found out that this new friend was not a true friend either. All of this happened in a span of three years.

This need for a special friend, one who would stick closer than a brother, was a deep longing in my heart. I would cry and pray, trying to figure out why no one measured up. So I eventually started giving up on hoping for that kind of friend because I could not find one who would love me for me. I wanted a friend who would stand by me through thick and thin, never talk bad behind my back, and not laugh at me or put me down in front of others. As I look back now, I understand that God was trying to show me He wanted me to know that I already had a friend like that because I had Him. He was that Friend that I was always looked for! What I realized later is that God was giving me a two-fold blessing. He helped me to understand that I needed Him in my life to show me what a true friend would be like. He had put this need for a friend in me to draw me to Himself. He was teaching me what a true friend looks like. Another thing that He was doing was He was teaching me to learn to give to those less fortunate than me. I learned to not be selfish or stingy and I can easily recognize others who are.

Just a few years ago I thought I had found such friend, and I got my hopes up once again as I did long ago. But I know now that God and only God can be the kind of friend to me that I long for most deeply.

A few years ago I had not yet completely come to this realization. It wasn't until recently that God revealed to me that only He could fill that emptiness inside of me. It was an emptiness that I wanted to fill with a friend. I tried to fill the emptiness with a boyfriend or a husband, but none of those worked either. God showed me that this was a special friendship that only He could fulfill in my life. Now finally I don't look for a special or close friend because I have one, His name is Jesus, and no one else can compare to Him. He is my Friend that will stick closer to me than a brother.

I said all of that to say this: we have a Friend in Jesus and the Holy Spirit. He will never leave us nor forsake us, the Bible tells us that in Hebrews 13:5. If we draw near to Him He will draw near to us – James 4:8.

EARLINE TERRELL CAMERON

Chapter Four

PROTECTION AND RESTORATION

That first summer in the white house I read my entire Bible. It may have even only been the New Testament, I am not sure, but I read it and prayed for help from God. As I continued to pray, God did show up and we were able to move to another house that was better. We lived in that unit for three years, then we moved to another house.

-- The Explosion and Fire –

--Miraculous Protection --

We lived in that fourth house for three years when tragedy happened. We used to have a big gas tank that sat out on the back of our house. Its purpose was to supply gas to our gas oven. One morning there was an explosion. The fire quickly spread throughout the four-room house. Two adults and three children were asleep inside. Fortunately the loud noise awaken them very suddenly and they were all able to get out alive and unharmed. Had it not been for the grace of God to awaken them from being sound asleep they could have been overcome by smoke, or with chaos and fear someone could have been left behind because they were all in different rooms. God's angels were there, however, and all got out safely and no one was harmed. All of our personal belongings, however, were destroyed in that consuming fire, but we thanked God for his protection over our lives!

After the fire, we moved a couple of doors down to another house. This was a green house. We would live here for two years. God was indeed setting us up to be able to buy a brand new house so we could finally stop moving from place to place. In this greenhouse I graduated from high school and was able to get a good job. This was not just any job, this was a job that many other people had put in for but were not able to get. I believe everyone in my family had put in for this job, but God blessed me to get it a year later. With the combined income of my mom, dad, my sister (who was married) and my income, we could afford a brand new house in the city. God is so good, this was one of the happiest times of my life.

-- The Bully --

I was taught by my mother that sisters and brothers are supposed to stick close together. We had to watch out for each other. I took my responsibility about what my mother said seriously.

Every day my mother reminded us as we would leave home to go to school to be sure and look out for each other. She would tell me to watch my little brother and not let anyone hurt him. In my thinking, as an eight or nine year old kid, this was my assigned job from my mother, and I took it very seriously, but it also caused me to feel a lot of pressure. I don't understand why my sister, who was two years older than me, wasn't given this task. Maybe her classroom was in another building. I don't know why, but this is what she told me to do and I watched over my brother as if my life depended on it. My mom never threatened me or anything, I just wanted to be obedient to what she told me to do.

All the years I watched over my brother while he was small, I had only one incident and this was with the big bully who rode on the bus. It was a late afternoon and we got on the bus coming back home as usual. Each seat on the bus was long enough to permit three people to sit on it at a time. I believe a person sat next to the window, I told my brother to sit in the middle, and then I sat on the outside next to the aisle.

The bully was a bit intimidating because of his looks and his height. His clothes were raggedy, his shoes were always too big and scuffed over. He was very loud and all the kids were afraid of him. Would you believe he sat in the row of seats behind our seats? I was looking straight ahead in front of me, not really paying attention to my brother because I had him in the middle so I could watch him. I had seated myself on the aisle as well so no one was going to step over me to hit him or anything. What I had not calculated on was that he could get hit from behind by someone sitting in the seat in back of us. I happened to look over at my brother, he had his head down sniffing and crying quietly. Then I heard a thump on his head, then another thump on his head. The bully was thumping him with his knuckles. God forbid, I jumped up, I looked at that bully and I screamed at him at the top of my voice! I said, "If you don't get your 'x,y,z' hands off my 'x,y,z' brother, I will kill you!" Until this day I don't recall his name, but that bully jumped backward and pointed at me and said, "Look at her, look at her!" I was highly upset to say the least. Interestingly, the bully never sat near my brother and I again after that encounter. He didn't walk anywhere near us; I don't think he bullied anyone else after that incident either.

As I look back at that situation, I think a twofold thing played out that day. God loves all of us. He loves the troublemaking bully as well. One, I think I was able to show my brother love and protection, demonstrating that I was there for him, and also to go home and tell my mom about the incident to let her know that I was obedient to what she told me – not to let anyone do him harm. She knew that bully would want to pick on him, which is why I had to protect him. He was my little brother and I had to stick close to him. The other thing that unfolded was that the bully stopped bullying the kids (even me). He acted more civil and was not as loud and obnoxious as he previously was. Had he continued to bully kids I would have known about it. He was exposed that day. I began to feel bad for him, he was a messed up kid himself. I'm pretty sure he had many issues. He was sort of slow, so was his sister, and he had to take care of her, but he never had any problems with kids because he was taller, louder, scarier, and very intimidating. The good news is that God used me as a blessing to protect my brother, but also to stop that young boy from becoming a disaster. God no doubt put fear in him to stop his patterns of bullying before someone got hurt or killed. I am glad, because I did not need to fight that boy with my pencil as scared as I was. I felt like a cat that was backed up against the wall, I was coming out with my brother safely, but God stepped in right in the nick of time. I don't know what kind of look was on my face, but he kept screaming "Look at her! Look at her!" and pointing at me. But I do know that the look put fear in his heart and he was a better kid after that. He would not sit near us on the bus for the rest of the school year! I thank God for being a blessing to this young boy so that he would stop his bullying ways. I am so amazed at how God used a little skinny fearful girl like me to do it, but I don't question God, He is God.

EARLINE TERRELL CAMERON

Chapter Five

LEARNING TO TRUST

What I have learned in life is that you get out of relationship with God what you put into it. If you don't put anything in it, you can't get anything out of it. God is with us every step of the way. Sometimes He lets us know that He is watching over us, sometimes we want to say "Where are you God?", but if you are chosen from the foundation of the world, and God has his hand on your life, you will be or do whatever He has called you to do. He may have to drag you, but you are coming. A lot of times we get off track with God when we start coming of age, we think that because we are a certain age, we can make decisions for ourselves, but believe me, He will not let you get away. Even if you think you have done too much wrong, or too many bad things and you are not deserving to be back in the will of God, you are still His child and He will never leave you nor forsake you. So you are "stuck", but you are in the best place!

I believe that if you are a child of God, He has called you from the foundation of the world. He knows before we are born what year we will become saved. Because God is omniscient He sees all. So in my case, I remember God's hand being on me throughout my life. I was not saved, as a matter of fact, I did not know much about God even though I believed in Him. I knew that I wanted to go to heaven and be with God when I died, therefore I wanted to do what was right, even though I did not always manage that very well. So, when God would help me when

I got in trouble, that made me know that He was watching over me. Often times I would cry and pray for a situation and God would show up and help me or bring me comfort.

As I look back on the tough times, the difficult times when I really thought that I was alone, I would then come to my senses and remember that God is always with me. God sustained me through the really bad times in my life when there were such big challenges, God was there for me. Sometimes we may be looking at our situation -- whatever it is -- maybe the scary diagnosis, the home foreclosure, or the car repo, and we forget to look at our God first. He is bigger than anything that we can think of. Psalms 142:45 says "I looked on my right hand and beheld, but there was no man that would know me; refuge failed me; no man cared for my soul. I cried unto Thee, O Lord; I said 'Thou art my refuge and my portion in the land of the living'." So we have to remember to look at our God, for He is always with us. He said He would never leave us nor forsake us.

God does miracles in our lives to help us believe and have faith. God knew that as He did all of these miracles in my life, when the time was right He would open my mind's eye and I would clearly see what He had been doing throughout my whole life. As a child of God, we are destined for greatness. We have a God-appointed destiny and there are God-appointed destinations for our lives. As individuals, our specific destiny may differ from another child of God, but each one of our destinies are God's best for *us*. Therefore, it should be our goal to be our best in serving Him.

In her book "Where Miracles Happen", Joan Wester Anderson quoted an article from Time Magazine,

December 30, 1991. The article stated *"'A miracle is a wonder, a beam of supernatural power injected into history.... It makes an opening in the wall that separates this world and another. "*

Miracles are not as scarce as some people think. God is assigning His angels to assist us every day, all day long.

Another definition of a miracle was found in the Webster's unabridged dictionary encyclopedia edition, which states *"A miracle is an event or effect that apparently contradicts known scientific laws, and is hence thought to be due to supernatural causes."*

Betty Malz, author of "Angels Watching Over Me", stated, *"It is not a miracle if you can explain it"*.

I cannot explain any of the miracles that God gave me because all of them were situations where it had to be God, it had to be supernatural because they are otherwise unexplainable.

God is continually revealing things to me regarding my purpose in life. He unfolds my past and my future right in front of my eyes. He does things in His own time. Since 2012, the Holy Spirit has revealed to me what the content of my book is supposed to be about. He has not revealed the name of the book yet, but I am sure by the end of the book He will reveal that to me as well.

In 1987 Fuller Theological Seminary wrote a document entitled "Ministry and the Miraculous". This document affirms that at that time a growing number of denominations were accepting that God does indeed work miraculously. This document states *"We must be transparently ready to submit our claims... to the most rigorous of empirical testing to guard against charlatans and hoaxes."*

All of these examples are proof that there is something to the fact that God still deals with people miraculously as He did in biblical times.

I thank God that He has shown me proof of His existence many times throughout my life. These experiences have in a sense given me such an inner peace, taking away my fear and giving me hope for the future. Therefore, when I think about these special times when God has given me these miracles, I feel

such intense joy for a while, and then I settle within myself and "come back to earth!". In the spaces in my life where I don't actually see God doing miracles I start to question what God is doing or why doesn't He hear me? But as always, He shows up in the right time. He so lovingly guides me and replenishes my faith. I am so sure that I am not alone. My appetite for God and His Word is so insatiable. I crave more and more of Him. I know that is what has bought me to this point.

How often do people stop to think about what it is they truly believe? Most of the time people never really give it a thought. They go about their business each day not being serious about who God is. I think one of the major dilemmas that face our society today as it relates to God is that our society doesn't think at all about who our Heavenly Father is, or what is required of us to be in a loving relationship with Him.

When we are in a relationship with God or with anyone for that matter, if that relationship means anything to us, we will try to find out how to cherish that relationship, how to keep it and honor it.

In my walk with God, I have learned that God speaks to me in a variety of ways. Sometimes it is through His Word, the Bible. Sometimes God speaks to me in my spirit. God speaks to His people in different ways; we have to be in tune with God to hear His voice.

Relationship with God is very important because there is no way that we can get to know the mind of God if we have no relationship with Him. Relationship helps us to get close to Him. This happens by daily studying His Word. We come to know Him and to love Him as our Father and that is what He wants. He chose us from the foundation of the world, He is omniscient and omnipresent, and so He knew us before we were born or thought of by anyone! Since He knows all, He also knew that after we were born on a certain date we would give our life to Him and do *His* will, not our own.

HIDDEN MIRACLES

Chapter Six

ANGELIC PROTECTION

I really truly believe God assigns angels to His people. I believe that God has assigned angels to me, to minister to and protect me and my children, grandchildren, and great grandchildren.

I remember when my oldest son was about five or six years old, he was trying to cross the street to get to the other side where his sister and friends were. He misjudged the closeness of the car coming down the street, and the car ran over him. I am not sure if the car hit him or not, but somehow he ended up under the car! I was at home at the time and I heard the kids outdoors screaming that my son had been hit by a car or had been run over. I remember being almost too weak to walk I was so full of fear. I was calling Jesus with everything in me. There was instant chaos. I made it to the street, which was only a few feet away, but it was a task to get there and the thoughts that were going through my head about what shape he was going to be in when I got there made me half blind with anxiety.

When I got outside the driver of the car was screaming and crying. She was in bad shape. She was pregnant and I was pregnant also. I looked and saw my son standing there dusting his pants off, smiling as if nothing had happened. He did not have a scratch on him! I was thanking God for saving my son! I still thank God for His protection over my boy every day of our lives! It was an absolute miracle!

God is an awesome God. I cannot say that enough. At that time I did not know much about God and how He deals with His people. I did not know anything about miracles or angels. But as I look back I can see how angels sent by God protect my children.

I remember a few years later when my son was in high school, he and his friend went on the wrong side of town and were shot at. My son and his friend left the apartment building and they were running for their lives! My son said a bullet went right by his ear. When he got home he told me what had happened, he was so scared and so glad to be home! He said he could feel the wind from the bullet pass his ear. God sent an angel to make sure my son got home safely, and I thank God for His protection for my child.

I know it's hard to believe, but I still did not get it, that God was protecting my son. I knew of God and I thought that I had a relationship with God, but the relationship that I had with God was different than the one I have now, because I am saved and filled with the Holy Spirit. I have more wisdom and I feel closer to God now.

- Brother and Children Protected –

- Gun Incident -

I remember years ago my younger brother had brought a gun home. I have no idea where he got the gun. My mom and dad were at work, I was at work too. No actual grown-ups were around at home. My younger sisters and brothers were there, and so were my children.

My brothers and sisters pointed the gun at each other and pulled the trigger so many times. My brother thought the gun was empty so they were acting out like actors do on T.V. in the movies. They would aim the gun, pull the trigger, and shoot at each other, then fall down pretending to be shot. They even pointed the gun at my children's heads as well. Finally, I believe it was my brother who had the gun, and this time he pointed the gun at the wall and the gun went off. Everyone was so terrified. They learned that day to never play with guns. Oh dear God the angels were busy that day! That one bullet was held jammed in that gun until it could come out safely, so that no one in that house would get hurt. It was really a testament of how far God will go to protect His people, especially if someone is praying, has a relationship with the Almighty God, and knows how to call on Him for protection for their family. He is faithful to do His part! I still did not think "miracle" even when that happened, but as I look back now I see clearly that was a protective miracle of God.

- Protection from Angry Boyfriend -

Years ago when my ex-husband was still only my boyfriend, God did another miracle in my life. We were having an argument of sorts. We had been next door with some friends and family. When we came home, I went into the bathroom because I was afraid that he would want to actually put his hand on me or be violent with me. He knocked really hard on the door. I opened it, he came in and closed the door behind him. He began to accuse me of some things and he started hitting me. I tried to protect myself the best way I could. I believe God sent His angels to intervene on my behalf. The next thing that happened in that little small bathroom was very sudden and swift. I was left really puzzled and it was hard to believe what had just occurred. My ex-husband had his back against the wall, I was standing in front of the sink, and there were only a few inches between us. He hit me and then he fell backwards, he went down and his head hit the floor and part of the wall at the bottom. He was knocked unconscious momentarily. I saw he was trying to shake it off. He was sort of smiling when I asked him if he was alright I was embarrassed and so was he. He got up and did not say a word. He went to the bedroom and a few minutes later when I thought about what had just happened I could not comprehend it. I was happy, but felt bad for him because he was upset over a situation that was so innocent. His insecurities caused him to look at and interpret the situation differently and he handled it poorly, but my God stepped in because He knew I was afraid and I could have been hurt or even killed right there in that tiny bathroom. I believe God stepped in on behalf of us both because it was a helpless situation going nowhere fast! If we can handle something ourselves there is no need for a miracle or for God to show up. In my case, in that bathroom, I was so afraid and in danger. The most High God showed up for me because I am His child.

- Brother Stabbed -

One might my brother was hanging with some of his friends or should I say buddies. An argument started between he and one of the buddies. My brother got stabbed under the arm near of the crucial veins near his heart. The doctor said another inch or half inch and my brother would have been dead. God sent an angel to move my brother just in time so that the stab would not be fatal. I know God did it and I thank Him even today for those miracles He did back then to save my family.

EARLINE TERRELL CAMERON

Chapter Seven

GOD HEARS AND ANSWERS PRAYER

-God Helps Crying Daughter –

I remember when my youngest daughter graduated from high school she worked at a couple of burger-stand jobs, then she finally got a more serious job where she worked in an office atmosphere. She had to dress nicely for that job and she was happy she made a little more money that she had at the burger stands.

I had just gotten saved around that time and I had started praying for my family members and anyone else that God would put on my mind more than I had every prayed before. One day my daughter was crying, telling me how mean the people were to her at her work and all the things that were going on. It seemed as though they were teaming up on her at work. I was so hurt for her, I prayed and cried out to God to correct the situation for her at her job. I could not understand how anyone could treat my daughter that way, she is such a sweet and loving child and always has been. I continued to go before the Lord on my daughter's behalf in prayer. About four or five days later I checked in on her to see how things at her work were. She said they were about the same. Those people did not like her.

About another week went by, I asked her again how things were at her job. She said, "Mom, they fired the big boss and all of the other supervisors under him, the one lady who continued to harass her was gone as well. They brought in a new management and my daughter was so happy! I thanked God for helping my daughter. He stepped in there and changed all of the people who were so corrupt and who were harassing her! That was a miracle because everyone was replaced at the same time. I was crying and thanking God for what He did, for hearing and answering my prayers so powerfully on her behalf!

-God Answers Prayers for Sister's Needs –

About another three weeks after my daughter's situation was over, my sister called me and told me that she was having some problems on her job also. Her supervisor and his whole team were harassing her. She was, I believe, afraid to go to work for fear of what these people would do.

Her supervisor had been inappropriate enough to hit her on her back with his fist! She was walking in front of him when he did that to her. I was so hurt when she told me, but I calmed her down and gave her some encouragement on what the Lord would do to help her. When I got off the phone I prayed and cried out to the Lord to help my sister in her situation. I continued to pray for her daily.

In about a week or so I called her to see how things were going. She said they were still harassing her and getting really bold at it. I continued to pray for her. After about two weeks or so I called her to check on her once more to see what was happening.

When she told me I was not surprised at all, because I saw what God had done for my daughter, and I know that He is no respecter of persons. She told me that the old management team got demoted. A new team came in, she filed papers against her old supervisor, they had to go to court, and he no longer worked at the company! I thank God for intervening for my sister. She is a good worker. God heard and answered my prayer on her behalf. God is still in the miracle working business. I love the Lord, He has been good to me and my loved ones!

-God Helps Me at My Job –

I have worked many jobs over the years. Some of the supervisors and managers have been very good people, some not-so-good. One of the not-so- good ones had a problem with me that I am not sure about still to this day. One day this person called me out in the area where I was working. Out of the blue they started screaming at me. Both he and my co-worker were in a heap of trouble. She was demoted for the rest of her tour of duty and he was demoted for a year to two years. He returned to work at another facility.

Again, God made a way out of no way for me. Even though this person was able to come back after two years, I had time to forgive them for the way they treated me and they were different because my co-worker was not in the mix. The harassment stopped when the two of them left. Praise God, the Lord knows how much we can take and He knew that I was at the end of my rope with all of the lying about me they were doing. That co-worker did their best to be sure I wouldn't have any kind of favor with my supervisor/manager. I had always tried to be nice and careful and friendly to my co-worker, but this person had a mean and jealous streak in them toward me that just could not be hidden. Some days were better than others, but for the most part they hated me for no reason. I would pray for the co-worker and my supervisor/manager, but finally one day my God said enough is enough and that was it! I praise God every day for bringing me out of that situation. The Lord has brought me out of many situations. I just cannot thank Him enough.

Chapter 8

MIRACLES OF RESTORATION AND HEALING

- A Friend Healed From Horrible Auto Injuries -

One night my son and his friend were driving back from an adjoining town. His other friend and one of his pals were in another car. It was late, and pretty dark down this street. His friend in the other car was ahead of my son and his friend by a distance of about half a mile down the road. As my son got closer to the city limits where the lights were, he could see that his friend and his pal had been in a terrific accident; their car was wrapped around an electric pole. My son and his friend called the police for help and the young men were taken to the nearest hospital The two young men were in critical condition, it was not known if they would survive through the night. One, then two days went by, and meanwhile everyone was praying. I didn't want to see my son's friend in the condition he was in.

On the third day they were still in critical condition and under a medically induced coma. My son's friend had not moved or shown any sign of trying to get better. My son kept calling me to come and see his friend. He was afraid he would not make it. I knew he was in bad shape, but I was praying and I believed God was going to bring his friend out of the coma. I wanted to wait until his friend got out of the hospital and came home, then I planned to go see him. But it seemed God had another plan. So, I went to the hospital and my son met me there. We went to his friend's room. He was lying in the bed looking so vulnerable and disfigured. I touched his leg slightly and started to pray. As soon as I started to pray my son's friend started moving his leg, then both legs, sort of like riding a bicycle. He started moaning and moving his arms and his head. My son got so scared he ran down the hospital corridor hollering for the nurses to come in to see about his friend. The nurse came in and asked what had happened. I told her I had touched his leg just slightly and he started moving like he was doing. She said, "He's okay, we want him to wake up and start moving. We have been waiting for this." The nurse was so glad my son's friend was moving. I was thanking God for touching that young man with mercy!

We left the room so the nurse could take care of him. I went down and talked with his mother and I felt that the Lord wanted me to tell her that "the seed of her womb was blessed." When I shared that with her it put her mind at peace. God is so awesome! Now when I see my son's friend, he does not look like that person that was lying in that hospital bed that day. God is so merciful, compassionate, and gracious towards us. "The Lord is compassionate and gracious, slow to anger, abounding in love" (Psalm 103:8)

- Miraculous Healing from a Stroke –

Another time God assured my family when I prayed for my nephew who, at the young age of forty, had a sudden stroke. My sister called me on the phone; she was crying so hard she could hardly talk. I consoled her the best I could and I told her not to worry, that God is able to heal and save him. I got off the phone with her and called my prayer partner (my daughter). She and I agreed over the phone in prayer, asking God to heal him and restore his body and mind.

The stroke had caused his mouth to become twisted to the side of his face and he had no feeling on his left side. He was totally paralyzed on the left side of his body. We prayed for him, believing that he was healed because that is what the Word says. There was no doubt in our minds that it was a done deal. A few hours later my sister called me back and she was so happy over the phone. She said, "I don't know what happened, but his mouth is not twisted up anymore, and his left side is not paralyzed anymore. Everything is just back the way it was before the stroke and he's totally normal!!!"

I told her that we prayed for God to completely restore him back to health. We prayed for the stroke to be reversed and God did exactly that! My nephew was on his way to recovery, thank God for healing for my nephew. The doctors said that they had never seen anything like it and said he was very lucky. I told everyone it had nothing to do with luck, but it was the grace of Almighty God, and Jesus still heals today. As a family, we knew this was truly a miracle from the Lord.

God performs miracles to get the attention of non-believers so they might be open to hearing the Gospel of Jesus Christ. I took this opportunity to talk to my sister about God. She seemed very receptive, but she is not totally convinced it was a real miracle. I am still working on her and I am sure the Holy Spirit is working on her heart as well.

– **Diagnosed with Cancer** –

I love to talk about the goodness of God and what He has done for me. Sometimes I just want to dance. I remember about six or seven months after I had graduated, they were hiring at a huge plant in my hometown. Everyone was trying to get a job there. I put in for it, as did most people. I got called for an interview, passed the interview and God blessed me with the job.

I went for the medical exam, which was required by the company as part of the hiring process. The doctor told me that I had cancer, but I didn't believe him. The doctor was our family doctor. He was the doctor that my family went to whenever we were sick. I had found out that he had cancer and I felt so bad for him, but I did not agree with him when he said I had cancer. It sort of shocked me, but I said "That's not true, the Lord just gave me this job and I will live to work it. Besides, I had to help my family move into a better house. When I prayed, I'm not sure how my prayer went, but I could have told that doctor that the Lord was directing my steps and I was going somewhere and had purpose for my life, so his diagnosis did not line up with what God was doing with me.

A few months later I met the person at work who God wanted me to meet. This person gave me some information that changed my entire life. She told me to fast and pray. I did and I met God, the God who had been with me all along, doing miracles for my family. So my God did not let me entertain the thought of cancer, because He was taking me somewhere. I was too busy pursuing God, so as I continued to seek Him with fasting and prayer He healed me and I did not even have to skip a beat!

Chapter Nine

GOD'S PROTECTION

On a Saturday afternoon I was driving on the freeway to my friend's house. I stayed in the slow lane because I did not want to drive too fast since I was not in a hurry. I noticed a person at the top of the embankment dressed in black. The person started out from behind the green barrier fencing and the concrete wall. He threw a shiny silver-colored object at my car. I knew that I did not have enough time to speed up or slow down. The object was coming straight at my windshield. The object was coming from the right side. All I could do was call Jesus and cover my face so that the glass from my windshield did not get into my eye. The miracle was that evidently my angel redirected the object because I was waiting for the object to hit, but it did not touch my windshield at all! Instead, very oddly, It came on my side of the car, hit my door, then drug alongside over the door handle, and dropped on the ground. I heard something fall, but I was too scared to look.

The person who threw that object watched for a couple of seconds to see if the object was on target. When I thought it would hit my windshield, he jumped back behind the concrete. What the enemy tried to use for evil, God used for good. God gave me this testimony to show me that I belonged to Him and I was His child and He would protect me. This testimony will help a lot of people believe and know that God is real and He does perform miracles even today. When I got to my friend's house, I stepped out of my car and looked at my vehicle for damage. I saw how the sharp object had hit the car upon impact and gouged my car.

- God Protects Me from Someone Shooting at My Car –

One night I was on my way to Bible study, got off on my exit, went down the ramp to a stop sign and stopped. I proceeded to the next stop sign, which was the large street that I was going to. I checked to the right and left, no cars were in sight, so I proceeded to make my right turn. As soon as I pulled out in the street I heard shots ring out. My back window of my car was blown out. I drove my car up on the sidewalk and into the drive-through lane at the fast food place there. I drove around past the drive-through window, jumped out, and the owner called the police for me. They interviewed me and then checked my car for the bullets. They looked for maybe fifteen to twenty minutes, and found no bullet holes! They walked over to me and asked me what happened to the bullets and I answered that I didn't know. I told them I got out of the car as soon as I could stop in safety. I told them that all I knew was that somebody shot at me and blew out the back window of my car. They could not find the bullets. For days I would go out to my car and check in places I thought I had missed, but the bullets were nowhere to be found! I can just see that angel redirecting that bullet or bullets! Certainly at least one had hit the window and blew out all the glass, but it did not come inside of my car where I was, because my God put a shield up all around me to protect me. He is a miracle working God! If you ask me why do I love God, my answer is not because of anything I've done, but because of what He has done for me. He is a miracle working God, even today. Yes, He performed miracles in the Bible, but He performs miracles right today as well, so I will never forget that night when I was trying to get out of the line of fire. To say I was very shook up would be an understatement. My heart was racing and I was afraid, but it was sort of like something out of the movies, very surreal. God is good, and I cannot thank Him enough for protecting me from harm or worse.

Don Jacobson, author of "It's a God Thing", says, *"I have to tell you that I believe in miracles. I believe in the miracles of the Bible, and I also believe that God is still doing miracles every day."* Mr. Jacobson tells of how he himself has had a bunch of miracles happen to him throughout the years.

On his blog with Fox News he stated, *"Miracles aren't a reward for good behavior. In fact, I don't think they're a reward at all. They are not all equal: some are small, almost imperceptible to all but the recipient. Others are jaw-on-the-floor big, with seemingly impossible events conspiring to bring about an inexplicable change of circumstance."*

I think people need encouragement and hope, because as you look around at this world we now live in, things don't look so uplifting. As a matter of fact, things look downright bleak or dark. When you share stories or testimonies about how God protected you or saved you from a disastrous situation, that uplifts people, they begin to have hope again, and know that if God did it for me He can do it for you, because He is not a respecter of persons.

-God Keeps My Car Running Supernaturally –

I remember one night I was driving home from church. It was late, I had a long way to drive home... the total distance was approximately seventy miles. When I was about half way home, my car started acting funny. The motor was making a noise and the car eventually started slowing down. The lights started flickering on and off too. I had to drive in the slow lane and pray. The car was very erratic in the way it was handling. It would speed up a bit and then slow down. I kept my foot on the gas, but it did not matter, the car would slow down anyway. When I still had about twenty miles left to go I began to get really afraid, because there weren't many cars out that time of night. Slowly I made my way until there were only about ten miles to go before I would be home. I asked the Lord to watch over me because I had heard stories about people driving the freeway up in that area just for the sake of looking for people to harm who were having car trouble.

I continued to drive the car, but it was getting worse by the minute. With five miles remaining before I would be home, the car was still running and I was praying up a storm! I came upon my exit, got off, and fortunately the light stayed green as I made the left turn. All of the lights stayed green from street to street as I made my way to my house. When I had been fifteen to twenty miles distance from home I had prayed "God, please don't let the car stop until I am safely at home in my own driveway." God honored my cry for help! I pulled up in my driveway, parked the car, and turned the motor off. I tried to start the car up again to check it, but the car would not start.

That car never started again after I turned it off! I continue to thank God for getting me home safely that night!

"Miracles happen every day. Not just in remote country villages or at holy sites half way across the globe, but here in our own lives, towns, cities" – Deepak Chopra (from very best quotes.com)

I believe miracles happen as a result of God dispatching angels to protect or rescue us. In the case of my car trouble on the freeway late that night, I believe angels were pushing that car, turning the lights back on when they went out, and keeping that motor running. I even think some went ahead of me to the street lights and made sure no lights would turn red so I could keep the car moving!

It was moving so slowly that when I came to the green lights to make the turns I never had to hit the brakes! My car was going so slowly I didn't even have to stop at the two stop signs either. My angels pushed me all the way home that night! God heard my prayer and sent those angels to protect me, His child, and bring me safely home. This was another testimony that God gave me to use to encourage His people.

Everything that He has done for me or given me is for me to use to be a blessing to others. He does not bless us for us to sit on the blessing and keep it to ourselves, but we are blessed to *be* a blessing.

In the book "The Boy Who Came Back From Heaven", Alex Malarkey says *"One night about two weeks after I came out of the coma, Daddy and a friend named Margaret were with me. I was tired and didn't feel like trying to answer questions, so Daddy and Margaret were just talking to each other. Then something happened. I saw angels in my room – they were everywhere."* Later in the book Alex shares *"I couldn't stop looking at them. The angels started to help me. Some of the angels put their hand on my chest and were helping me to breathe. Other angels started to help me talk. I started to try to make words with my mouth and all of a sudden I said 'Mom'. When that word came out, I was very happy and said it over and over."* Kevin and Alex Malarkey, from Alex "Angels Keeping me" chapter 6, page 115-116).

- Asleep at the Wheel: Miraculous Protection -

There was another incident, also late at night, when I was driving home from church, and I was a little sleepy. As I was getting closer to home the sleepiness got worse and it was all I could manage to stay awake. My drive was about an hour and twenty minutes in length, so it was a challenge to stay awake. I turned the music up loud, let the windows down for a while, chewed gum, all of those things along with praying to fight being overcome by sleepiness. I remember being about five miles from my exit on the road, then finally about a mile to go to my exit, but then I don't remember anything else until I was over a half mile *past* my exit and coming up on the next exit! I sort of "came to" and said something like "Jesus, where AM I?"

I immediately recognized the lights and the tall fence to my right, letting me know that I was coming up on the exit *past* my exit. I began to thank God for keeping me safe while I was literally asleep and driving. I believe the angels guided my car while I was asleep and gave me back control when I woke up. I was asleep only about maybe five to eight minutes or so, but so much could have happened in those few minutes, yet God kept me while I had clearly been asleep. It is so hard for me to think about being asleep for that amount of time while behind the wheel. The angels truly watched over me there, as well as the people around me as I was driving. The car must have been full of angels and surrounded by angels as well. I give God praise!

EARLINE TERRELL CAMERON

Chapter Ten

PROVISION AND GROWTH

- A Journey of Faith and Growth -

Miracles are happening all around us, but not everyone is privileged to recognize them. Sometimes you can see them, but nothing clicks in your understanding about it at the time. God allows you to be right there but not recognize what you are seeing is a miracle. He has been with me all of my life growing up, showing me miracles, but I did not know Him personally in my heart yet. I would pray and I knew He was with me, but I knew nothing about being saved, sanctified, and filled with His Holy Spirit.

I was called by God and I did not have a clue. I went to church every Sunday as a child and I enjoyed being at church, but I never could understand what the pastor was saying or what it meant. The only thing I remember him saying was "Father, I stretch my hands out to Thee, no other help do I know." That was his favorite saying. He meant well, but I just did not understand what he was saying! He was a Baptist preacher, and he did whoop and holler a lot. Although I did not understand a word he was saying I respected him tremendously. I thought this was the way preaching was, so it was ok. As I think about it, I remember the preacher would say, "It takes a made up mind." Way back then I did not fully understand this as a child, but I always wanted to make my mind up to do what was right, never-the-less I would go right back out and do wrong. As Paul said in Romans 7:19, "For the good that I would I do not, but the evil which I would not, that I do."

- Regular Church Attendance
Causes Spiritual Growth -

I went to several different churches on down the years, but the God of my youth was not in all of the churches that I attended. Finally I left church attendance all together and just stayed at home, watching preachers on the television. But the Lord continued to speak to me about having a church home, so I found a church where I was really learning the Bible for the first time, things about God that I did not know.

From my background I was not a person who studied the Bible. I knew God, but not His Word. I would read the Bible, but I did not know what I was reading. I could not really understand it. I have always had the King James Bible, but it was a little hard for me to understand. As I progressed in this church I tried to get everything out of my life that was not right. So for years I tried, but I continued to fall at some point or another. Sometimes it would take five, six, seven years of what I called doing good, then I would have a mishap.

I was growing in my love for the Lord. I knew that I had to stay in church and learn all that I could so that I would please God and be a blessing to my entire family. So, I settled into a permanent church environment and really began praising God. My growth launched forward suddenly as a result; I just wanted to worship God and get even closer to Him. I was raising my hands and crying and worshipping God every Sunday and every Wednesday evening as well as in my car.

- Learning About the Holy Spirit -

Miracles are happening all around us, but in order to actually recognize them for what they are, you really need to be in tune to the Holy Spirit. I say that because for years I was not in tune with what God was doing, therefore it just seemed like it was just things happened by chance. The tunnel-vision minded person cannot comprehend the spiritual things of God, nor believe them. That is the reason Jesus said in John 16:7 "But I tell you the truth: it is for your good that I am going away. Unless I go away the Comforter will not come to you, but if I go, I will send Him to you." So Jesus made it clear it was expedient that He return to the Heavenly Father so the He could send us the Holy Spirit in His place. While Jesus' spirit was incased in His human body, He was like us, in that He could only be one place at a time. But once He returned to the Heavenly Father He released His Spirit, Who has the ability to be everywhere He is needed all at the same time and available to all, all at the same time! It's wonderful!

We cannot know the things of God on our own. We need help from the Holy Spirit to appropriately discern when God is on the scene. I Corinthians 2:14 says "The man without the Spirit does not accept the things that come from the Spirit of God, for they are foolishness to him, and he cannot understand them because they are spiritually discerned." So, when these miracles were happening, I really couldn't not see them for what they were. It wasn't until 2012 that the Lord took the scales off my eyes (spiritually speaking) so that I could see spiritually what God had been doing all along on my behalf, and what He is still doing today.

You hear a lot of Christians say that the Holy Spirit is a "gentleman", and that is so true. He does not rush anything on you. He is so gentle and He will move at a pace that is right for you.

-- Gentle Holy Spirit --

I remember a few years back I prayed for the Holy Spirit to come upon me. As I prayed I wanted the Holy Spirit even though I was a bit scared to fall out all over the floor. It is so amazing what the Holy Spirit did to show me exactly how gentle He could be. One morning I woke up and as I went through the day I closed my eyes and saw the outline of a little fountain. The water was going up and out just a like a fountain. Even when I closed my eyes at night the little fountain was still there. I got so used to seeing it that I missed it when it left me. It was with me either two or three weeks. I remember when it came I told one of my friends at church that I was seeing a little fountain spring up in my head when I closed my eyes. Actually, it was in my eyes. She said "Wow, somebody is going to get the Holy Spirit!" I had already thought about this and felt that the Holy Spirit was easing His Spirit into me, and He did. He now lives inside of me, so I am filled with the Holy Spirit and speak in tongues, and I am sold out for Jesus.

As I continued to grow in my spirituality, I always wondered why I never fit in or why so many people were against me for no reason. A lot of times when we're going through some testing experience, it is so hard to see God's hand in the matter. However, we have to remember that God is always working His perfect will out for our sake. He can even turn evil to our good if we ask what He would like to teach us. Adversity works to strengthen us at the very core of our character, even though at the time when it comes we do not welcome it in our lives!

I remember when I got filled with the Holy Spirit. I was at church, everyone was praying, the person facilitating the work shop asked if anyone wanted to be filled with the Holy Spirit. They told us to stand up if we did and raise our hands and start speaking in a Heavenly language. I opened my mouth and started speaking in other tongues right away. It was so gentle, I was so at peace with it! I thought something like a jarring or a swift wind or something like that would happen, but that did not happen at all. So it really is true, the Holy Spirit is a gentleman, so loving and patient, you can sense His peace when He shows up or comes upon you. You just know that He loves you and will take care of you.

I learned about how being saved works in a life from one of my old classmates when I was in my twenties. She became my neighbor. I had not seen her in quite a while, until she and her husband and child moved in across the street. I met her sister-in-law at my job. I had seen her in high school and I heard that she was sanctified. She and I introduced ourselves and started chatting regularly. We got to be good friends.

I found out that my friend was now Spirit-filled as well. I knew nothing about being sanctified (set apart for God), but I would visit her almost every day just to hear what she had to say about God. I was Baptist, but not attending church as I should at that time. I believe this was divine intervention because I probably would not have ever talked to her at my job if her sister-in-law had not told me about her. When God put her in my life my entire life changed! She was the first person to tell me about fasting. I had never heard of it. One day I was feeling really bad over a situation. She told me to fast and pray about the problem. I fasted from 6 a.m. to 6 p.m. That was the hardest thing for me to do because I kept thinking about food! I would pray some, then food was on my mind again! I didn't think I would ever make fasting a part of my life. So much has happened since that day. It took me a long time to get to where I am today. I have been through a lot. I just think about how patient God is. It is so amazing how He just lets us make our choices in life, but if you are set apart and you belong to Him, you will eventually get it and He will be right there waiting!

As I look back on this situation, I am positive that when God puts a new person in your life it is to change your season. God heard my prayer and changed the direction of my life because of meeting that woman. As I look back now, I see how He let me make choices and He worked with me from where I was. But all the time He was bringing me or drawing me to Himself slowly. First He made sure that I recognized Him as a child, eleven and twelve years old, so as a twenty-one-year-old I could recognize Him again and know that He was my God and He was watching over me and my children throughout the years.

SUMMARY AND CLOSING

-Discovering Strengths and Patterns –

I remember my first year in Seminary, we were given a chance to see where our strengths and weaknesses were as it related to our ministry. I scored really high on giving, as a matter of fact, giving was double and almost triple the other gifts. I have the gift of giving because God started training me a long time ago. I love giving to those unfortunate ones who God has assigned me to be a blessing to. I cannot wait to give my first one thousand dollar seed. I think I am going to shout that glorious day!

I know God chose me from the foundation of the world. I know He is working His purposes in me, He is working some things *in* me, and working other things *out* of me! He is loving and faithful in the process. He has not given up on me, so I know He will not give up on you! God has been very patient with me, and I thank Him every day for His mercy and grace toward me and my entire family.

I was reading an article published back in November 2007 by Michael Fackerell on his website. The article said, *"Should it surprise a true believer in God that God is working miracles today? According to the Bible, Jesus Christ is the same yesterday, today, and forever – Hebrews 13:8. If Jesus was ever a miracle worker, He is today."* I thought that was interesting, because it is so true. God does not change. The Bible says in Malachi 3:6 "I am the Lord, I change not." To me it is so clear that God is truly performing miracles in the lives of His people every day.

I believe God started doing miracles in my family a long

time ago, when I was nearly twelve years old. I am sure it started even longer ago than that, but no one in my generation or no one in my parents' generation was praying, God will look in a generation and see who has a heart pliable enough which He can continue to bless and will raise up the ones who have a heart for Him.

Examples of this are given in the Bible too. Sometimes generation after generation is skipped, with nobody in the family line having a heart open to or receptive to God, and then finally there is one such as in the case of some of the kings in the Bible. After the death of King David, his son King Solomon reigned over God's people Israel. When Solomon inherited the throne, it was the most powerful kingdom then existing. It was a time of peace and prosperity.

God told Solomon to ask what he would and Solomon asked for wisdom to govern God's people. Solomon's request so pleased God that He richly rewarded Solomon with wealth, wisdom, power, and the important task of building the temple for God. (I Chronicles 28:2-6).

After Solomon's death, the kingdom of God's people Israel became divided. Ten tribes formed the northern kingdom which was called Israel; the tribes of Judah and Benjamin formed the southern kingdom which was then called Judah. All of the next kings that rose up in the northern kingdom of Israel practiced idolatry, Baal being the worst "god" they worshipped and made sacrifices to. Some of the kings of Judah served idols too, but others rose up and served God faithfully. Rehoboam was mostly a bad king of Judah; the king after him, Abijah, was mostly bad too. The next king Asa was a good king and so was his son Jehoshaphat, but the next kings four kings that followed were Godless. Finally along came King Asa who served and pleased God. He trusted God, he had an attitude and desire to please God wholeheartedly, therefore this resulted in blessings for King Asa and his people. So the Kingdoms of Judah enjoyed many years of peace and prosperity.

In modern times, if our ways please God He blesses us in many ways. The Bible says "Draw near to God and He will draw near to you." (James 4:8). God actually really does *want* to bless us, He has chosen us from the foundation of the world. He has given us a purpose in life. He wants to use us in the kingdom to be a mouthpiece for Him for such a time as this.

- God Moves in Our Lives for His Purposes -

I am learning that when God has His hands on you, He will do whatever He has to do to bring you to your intended destiny. He loves us just that much, and will chase us at times, but still He is sensitive to how much we can take.

I had it rough during my teen years and after, but the good news is that God did not give up on me and He won't give up on you either! He knows us. He knows what we are made of. I am so glad that He reads our hearts. He is such a loving God and He protects his people.

He is the Potter, we are the clay. He is always moving us, shaping us, molding us into what He has called us to be. What we look like today is not who or what He has called us to look like in our destiny. When He is done with us, we will look totally different. The Bible tells us that when we got born-again we were made new in Christ. Slowly He is moving us in that direction. I remember the song we used to sing which says "I looked at my feet, my feet looked new. I looked at my hands, my hands looked new." In actuality they appeared just the same on the outside, but everything was new on the inside, so it impacted everything else.

So as I amen this journey in my life, I realize that what God was birthing in me was the gift of giving. I am a giver, not a taker. I give, give, give, and I have joy in the giving. God produced this wonderful gift inside of me. As we go through life, especially if the Lord is going to use us, we will need to go through some things. He can't use us in the state that we're in. He wants to get ahold of us and work on us to bring us into the image of His own Son. The Bible tells us to be transformed by the renewing of our minds. Therefore our minds have to be renewed, so He works with us for years and years as He did and is still doing with me. I have learned that in every single trial or situation, there is a lesson to be learned. We just don't go through these things for nothing, there is a reason.

I trust God that these miracles and stories I have shared about God's goodness in my own life will be able to help other people to look at their lives as well, to see what God has done for them. I hope they too will get a revelation as to who He is and what He wants to do through them.

If you are a child of God, He has been following you throughout your life. On Facebook and Twitter you may have hundreds of followers, some people may even have thousands, but remember that Jesus was your first follower! I know we have been told to be a follower of Jesus Christ, and that's true, but we love Him because He first loved us! *He followed us before we followed Him!*

If you are a child of God, you can look back and see how He has strategically moved in your life, how He moved things out of the way. He put things and people in your life at just the right time. You can see how as you look back at the things that just had to be a miracle for it to happen or come to pass the way it did. Take the time to reflect and you will begin to realize that what I am saying is true! He will remove the scales from your eyes and you will see it for yourself.

A lot of people may want God to let them see their miracles, but for that to happen you have to be ready to walk in your destiny. He takes the veil off your understanding and gives you "eyes to see" so that you will know which way He wants you to go and what He wants you to do. He will show you the right direction, He will reveal to you what your particular ministry is. It will be an unfolding within your understanding. So child of God, get ready for your miracle.

I have found out that a lot of times the Holy Spirit speaks in our heart and tells us to do something, but we feel it is may be so big and overwhelming that we think that we cannot do it. When He does this we have to receive it and believe it will come to pass. It might not happen tomorrow or the day after, or even in the next year, but if we wait on Him and seek Him, He will unfold it and bring it to pass.

Wait on Him and He will begin to move in your life. He does not move when we say move, He moves in His own good time. Worship Him every day throughout the day. Learn to trust Him and develop a relationship with the Holy Spirit. He will be your best Friend if He is not yet already.

God is always trying to bless us so He works at our pace pretty much. He is working things in us and out of us so that He can use us. That is why He doesn't drop the whole dream or vision into our lap all at one time! There is a process that He will work out in you, so be ready to grow and praise Him in the midst.

Though we have many setbacks in our lives we must still move forward in God. A lot of times God tries to warn us not to do something, or not to go a certain route, but we do it our own way. That doesn't mean that God is mad that we made the wrong choice. Sometimes He has to create a miracle to save us, but still there are consequences for not obeying Him or not picking the choice or the way that He had mapped out for us. The miracle He provides is to save and protect us because He has called us from the foundation of the world. He will save you if He has to run you out of the club, drag you from the casino, whatever He has to do, He will do it. When you are chosen, He chastens His own.

God is looking for people who He can promote to higher levels of service. He looks for people who are willing to put Him first in their lives. You can't put anyone above Him. He is God Almighty! He is the Creator of all things. He cannot be put in second place to anyone or anything

In this walk with God, our tests and trials come to make us strong. We have to trust God that He will bring us out of the situation. Stay humble and encourage yourself in Him. Sometimes when we are going through things, it seems as though He has left us or He is not speaking to us. We may feel lonely, sad, unloved. Our feelings can be all mixed up, but this is not the time to give up, because He is faithful and He knows what we need. So at the right time He will show up and bring us through, but not before it is His time. He is molding and shaping us into that person who He has called. He is the Potter and we are His clay to mold and shape.

I thank God for all of my trials and tests, because they have made me stronger. The have helped me to gain wisdom and knowledge. I love God because he knows what we need and when we need it. He is a miracle-working God. We will understand that He is able to do anything.

I even thank God for the "haters" in my life. I do believe that God allows people in our lives to irritate us to actually get on our nerves every day so that patience will develop in us and we will learn to intercede in prayer and trust Him. What we discover is the circumstances may not change, or the problem person may still be in our life, but now because of God working in us we see things differently. The things that bothered us previously no longer do, because God has done a work in us. He will even give us love toward them, an ability to forgive them and see them with the eyes of His grace. We will gain compassion and hurt for them because they don't know how to move within the love of God in their own lives. The Bible tells us that God wants everyone to be saved. Yes, we have to pray for those who act as if they wish to be our enemy, so that they can get strength from God to have their hearts changed and softened, just as He has done in us.

A lot of us can look back on our lives and wonder why God did not call one of our siblings instead of us. Some of them look better, seem to have a better personality, or may even be smarter! So you may wonder why did He call you instead? To be honest, there are people that God will not choose to promote. The Bible tells us to "Set our affections on things that are above and not on things here below." Therefore, we must put God first in our lives. God has to be our top priority. That is the main quality that God is looking for in a person. Sometimes we put our children, husband, boyfriend, manager, supervisor, or whoever first, or before God. The fact that we let our supervisor persuade us to lie or tell untruths on our papers on the job, or let our friend convince us to lie for them or let our child do things that are not appropriate for teenagers all means we are putting them above the righteousness of God! When Jesus is Lord of your life, you put Him first above all else – above your child, mother, father, brother, friend, whoever.

Even historically, in the case of King David, God chose him over his older and good-looking brothers because God looks at the heart. He is not looking so much at the appearance. David's oldest brother probably should have been the pick of the sons if God had only been looking at appearance.

Even after God chooses us there is a process, it is not over night! You will have to endure pain, loneliness, rejection, hatred, ridicule, heartache, shame, harassment, and the list goes on. Sometimes these things come at the hand of those who are supposed to love us or be our friend. The enemy will try to assign people to you to discourage you and get your eyes off God and His ways. Never stop keeping your eyes on God, because when you come out of it you will know more about God and be stronger too. You will be a better person, a better servant of God now than you would have been had you not gone through anything difficult. God knows if you are ready to be used by Him. He waits until you are ready, not a day before!

If we are asking He will remove the blinders at some place and time for each of us. For me it wasn't until I was ready to do His will. Now that I have this information I can go forward with the plan that God has for my life. I just need to step out in faith, because nothing will happen until I make a move. Now that I am nearing the end of this book, I will be stepping out in faith, and I will pursue everything else that He has put in my heart to do. I believe fasting and prayer is key. It is so important to seek God for direction before making that move though.

Often when God tells you to perform a task it seems He is making sure the task is overwhelming to you! If feels as if there is no way you can do what He has put before you. You become very aware of your own smallness. But we have to have faith and believe that some way, somehow as we look to Him He is going to do what He has directed us toward.

Take a look at Abraham's life in the Bible. At ninety years of age God told him that he would be a father of many nations. Abraham was overwhelmed and didn't see how that could be possible because his wife had been barren and she was past childbearing age.

We can look again at King David as well. He had been proclaimed to be anointed as the future King over Israel by the prophet, but he had to wait seventeen more years before he actually became King! For each person called there appears to be a process that they will have to go through.

In 2008 when I heard in my spirit that I was supposed to write a book and start my business I had no idea how to do this. I was completely overwhelmed. It seemed that God just stopped speaking then because I was so unwilling and closed to the whole idea. But be assured, if God is the one putting something within you, He will bring it around again and again to your thoughts, whether you think you can do it or not! You will have to step out and trust Him and have faith in what He is telling you. You won't get all the answers at one time, but you will get enough to put your foot forward to take that single first step. You may think you are losing your mind, but the process is being worked within you and you are actually becoming stronger in God. He begins to open doors and makes a way where there was no way before!

Sometimes I sit and wonder why God calls the most unlikely person to the five-fold ministry, especially as it relates to families. I would have thought one of my older sisters would have been called rather than me. I made so many mistakes and felt so unqualified. But I do recall from early childhood on, I was the one who seemed to have such a reverent fear of the Lord. I wanted to do all that I could so that my family would be saved from the fires of hell. From that time until now I just have felt that God held me responsible to help my family and to stand in the gap for them in intercessory prayer. I have always prayed diligently for them, and God has faithfully heard my prayers and answered them.

I have written this book to encourage those who have been in situations similar to mine, and also for people out there who don't feel they have ever seen a move of God in their own lives. I want them to know that God is always busy behind the scenes, working to touch lives, protect, teach, guide, and do miracles on behalf of those who need Him. He is always saving individuals and families for His Glory.

I love God, He is my Father, my God, my Lord, my Savior, Deliverer, Redeemer, Way-Maker, my Lawyer, Advocate, Accounting Advisor, my Hope, my Peace, my "Knight in Shining Armor"; my Healer, Representative, Help and Strengthener, my Refuge.... He is my Everything! I worship Him and Him alone, there is no one else like Him. He is the only true and living God. He is the creator of the entire world. There is no one higher than He!

I hope that the sharing of my story in this book will encourage other people about God. I hope this will stir you to reflect on your own life, and to ask for His perspectives about your life so you too can see that Almighty God has been working on your behalf all along, whether you realized it or not! Many things that have happened have not been due to luck or coincidence, but have actually been God at work on your behalf. You may find that your own life has indeed been full of miracles unaware, and you may realize you even have your own story to write about His goodness. He loves each one of us so much and He will do whatever it takes to save us.

God Bless you.

EARLINE TERRELL CAMERON

www.ingramcontent.com/pod-product-compliance
Lightning Source LLC
LaVergne TN
LVHW021617080426
835510LV00019B/2627